Windows 10 Shortcut Keys.

By

U. C-Abel Books.

Table of Contents

Chapter three: Windows 10 Shortcut Keys (Using Apps)...28

INTRODUCTION

Wplane that astonishes people around us when we work e enjoy using shortcuts because they set us on a high with them. As wonderful shortcuts users, the worst eyesore we witness in computer operation is to see somebody sluggishly struggling to execute a task through mouse usage when in actual sense shortcuts will help to save that person time. Most people have asked us to help them with a list of keyboard shortcuts that can make them work as smartly as we do and that drove us into research to broaden our knowledge and truly help them as they demanded, that is the reason for the existence of this book. It is a great tool for lovers of shortcuts, and those who want to join the group.

Most times the things we love don't come by easily. It is our love for keyboard shortcuts that made us to bear long sleepless nights like owls just to make sure we get the best out of it, and it is the best we got that we are sharing with you in this book. You cannot be the same at computing after reading this book. The time you entrusted to our care is an expensive possession and we promise not to mess it up.

Your computing style will not be complete without the use of shortcuts. I advise you improve your style today.

Learn the **fifteen (15) keyboard shortcuts** every computer user should know, shortcut keys to use in **windows** 10 and the ones to use in its **apps**.

Thank you!

Acknowledgement.

U. C-Abel Books will not take all the credits for the shortcuts listed in this book, but will share them with Microsoft Corporation because most of the shortcuts came from them and "are used with permission from Microsoft".

What is New in this Windows 10 Shortcut Keys Book.

Take a look below to see the new list of shortcut keys in Microsoft Window and Apps contained in this book that other Windows Shortcut Keys in this series do not contain.

In Windows 10

1. 15 (Fifteen) keyboard shortcuts every computer user should know.
2. Command Prompt keyboard shortcuts
3. Virtual Desktop keyboard shortcuts

In Windows Apps

1. Settings keyboard shortcuts
2. Microsoft Edge keyboard shortcuts
3. Game Bar keyboard shortcuts
4. Photos Apps keyboard shortcuts

CHAPTER ONE

15 (Fifteen) Special Keyboard Shortcuts.

The fifteen special keyboard shortcuts are fifteen (15) shortcut keys every computer user should know.

The following table contains the list of keyboard shortcuts every computer user should know.

1. **Ctrl + A:** Control plus A, highlights or selects everything you have in the environment where you are working.

    If you are like **"Wow, the content of this document is large and there is no time to select all of it, besides, it's going to mount pressure on my computer?"** *Using the mouse for this is an outdated method of handling a task like selecting all, Ctrl+A will take care of that a second.*

2. **Ctrl + C:** Control plus C copies any highlighted or selected element within the work environment.

    Saves the time and stress which would have been used to right click and click again just to copy. Use ctrl+c.

3. **Ctrl + N:** Control plus N opens a new window.
   Instead of clicking **File, New, blank/ template** *and another* **click,** *just press* **Ctrl + N** *and a fresh window will appear instantly.*

4. **Ctrl + O:** Control plus O opens a new program.
   Use ctrl +O when you want to locate / open a file or program.

5. **Ctrl + P:** Control plus P prints the active document.
   Always use this to locate the printer dialog box and print.

6. **Ctrl + S:** Control plus S saves a new document or file and changes made by the user.
   Please stop! Don't use the mouse. Just press Ctrl+S and everything will be saved.

7. **Ctrl +V:** Control plus V pastes copied elements into the active area of the program in use.
   Using ctrl+V in a case like this Saves the time and stress of right clicking and clicking again just to paste.

8. **Ctrl + W:** Control plus W is used to close the page you are working on when you want to leave the work environment.

"There is a way Peace does this without using the mouse. Oh my God, why didn't I learn it then?" Don't worry, I have the answer, Peace presses Ctrl+W to close active windows.

9.   **Ctrl + X:** Control plus X cuts elements (making the elements to disappear from their original place). The difference between cutting and deleting elements is that in Cutting, what was cut doesn't get lost permanently but prepares itself so that it can be pasted in another location selected by the user.

> *Use ctrl+x when you think* ***"this shouldn't be here and I can't stand the stress of retyping or redesigning it in the rightful place it belongs".***

10. **Ctrl + Y:** Control plus Y redoes an undone action.

> *Ctrl+Z brought back what you didn't need? Press Ctrl+ Y to remove it again.*

11. **Ctrl + Z:** Control plus Z undoes actions.
> *Can't find what you typed now or a picture you inserted, it suddenly disappeared or you mistakenly removed it? Press Ctrl+Z to bring it back.*

12. **Alt + F4:** Alternative plus F4 closes active windows or items.

> *You don't need to move the mouse in order to close an active window, just press **Alt + F4** if you are done or don't want somebody who is coming to see what you are doing.*

13. **Ctrl + F6:** Control plus F6 Navigates between open windows, making it possible for a user to see what is happening in windows that are active.

> *Are you working in Microsoft Word and want to find out if the other active window where your browser is loading a page is still progressing? Use Ctrl + F6.*

14. **F1:** This displays the help window.

> *Is your computer malfunctioning? Use **F1** to find help when you don't know what next to do.*

15. **F12:** This enables user to make changes to an already saved document.

> *F12 is the shortcut to use when you want to change the format in which you saved your existing document, password it, change its name, change the file location or destination, or make other changes to it. It will save your time.*

Short Forms Used in This Book and Their Full Meaning.

The following are short form of Keyboard shortcuts used in this book, Windows 10 Shortcut Keys, and their full meaning.

1. Alt - Alternate Key
2. F - Shift Key
3. Ctrl - Control Key
4. Shft - Shift Key
5. Win - Windows logo key
6. Tab - Tabulate Key
7. Num Lock - Number Lock Key
8. Esc - Escape Key
9. Caps Lock - Caps Lock Key

CHAPTER TWO
Windows 10 Shortcut Keys
(Using Windows 10).

Top Keyboard Shortcuts

The following table contains common keyboard shortcuts for Windows 10.

Shortcut	Action
Ctrl+C (or Ctrl+Insert)	Copy the selected item
Ctrl+X	Cut the selected item
Ctrl+V (or Shift+Insert)	Paste the selected item
Ctrl+Z	Undo an action
Alt+Tab	Switch between open apps
Alt+F4	Close the active item, or exit the active app
Windows logo key ⊞+L	Lock your PC or switch accounts
Windows logo key ⊞+D	Display and hide the desktop

New Keyboard Shortcuts

The following table contains new keyboard shortcuts that you can use in Windows.

Shortcut	Action
Windows logo key ⊞+A	Open Action center
Windows logo key ⊞+S	Open search
Windows logo key ⊞+C	Open Cortana in listening mode **Note** • Cortana is only available in certain countries/regions, and some Cortana features might not be available everywhere. If Cortana isn't available or is turned off, you can still use search.
Windows logo key ⊞+Tab	Open Task view
Windows logo key ⊞ +Ctrl+D	Add a virtual desktop
Windows logo key ⊞ +Ctrl+Right arrow	Switch between virtual desktops you've created on the right

Windows logo key ⊞ +Ctrl+Left arrow	Switch between virtual desktops you've created on the left
Windows logo key ⊞ +Ctrl+F4	Close the virtual desktop you're using

General Keyboard Shortcuts

The following table contains general keyboard shortcuts in Windows.

Shortcut	Action
F2	Rename the selected item
F3	Search for a file or folder in File Explorer
F4	Display the address bar list in File Explorer
F5	Refresh the active window
F6	Cycle through screen elements in a window or on the desktop
F10	Activate the Menu bar in the active app
Alt+F4	Close the active item, or exit the active app
Alt+Esc	Cycle through items in the order in which they were opened
Alt+underlined letter	Perform the command for that letter
Alt+Enter	Display properties for the selected item
Alt+Spacebar	Open the shortcut menu for the active window
Alt+Left arrow	Go back
Alt+Right arrow	Go forward
Alt+Page Up	Move up one screen
Alt+Page Down	Move down one screen

Alt+Tab	Switch between open apps
Ctrl+F4	Close the active document (in apps that are full-screen and allow you to have multiple documents open simultaneously)
Ctrl+A	Select all items in a document or window
Ctrl+C (or Ctrl+Insert)	Copy the selected item
Ctrl+D (or Delete)	Delete the selected item and move it to the Recycle Bin
Ctrl+R (or F5)	Refresh the active window
Ctrl+V (or Shift+Insert)	Paste the selected item
Ctrl+X	Cut the selected item
Ctrl+Y	Redo an action
Ctrl+Z	Undo an action
Ctrl+Right arrow	Move the cursor to the beginning of the next word
Ctrl+Left arrow	Move the cursor to the beginning of the previous word
Ctrl+Down arrow	Move the cursor to the beginning of the next paragraph
Ctrl+Up arrow	Move the cursor to the beginning of the previous paragraph
Ctrl+Alt+Tab	Use the arrow keys to switch between all open apps

Ctrl+arrow key (to move to an item)+Spacebar	Select multiple individual items in a window or on the desktop
Ctrl+Shift with an arrow key	Select a block of text
Ctrl+Esc	Open Start
Ctrl+Shift+Esc	Open Task Manager
Ctrl+Shift	Switch the keyboard layout when multiple keyboard layouts are available
Ctrl+Spacebar	Turn the Chinese input method editor (IME) on or off
Shift+F10	Display the shortcut menu for the selected item
Shift with any arrow key	Select more than one item in a window or on the desktop, or select text within a document
Shift+Delete	Delete the selected item without moving it to the Recycle Bin first
Right arrow	Open the next menu to the right, or open a submenu
Left arrow	Open the next menu to the left, or close a submenu
Esc	Stop or leave the current task

Windows Logo Key Keyboard Shortcuts

A key on Microsoft Computer keyboard with its logo displayed on it. Search for this ⊞ on your keyboard.

The following table contains keyboard shortcuts that use the Windows logo key ⊞.

Shortcut	Action
Windows logo key ⊞	Open or close Start
Windows logo key ⊞ +A	Open Action center
Windows logo key ⊞ +B	Set focus in the notification area
Windows logo key ⊞ +C	Open Cortana in listening mode **Note** • Cortana is only available in certain countries/regions, and some Cortana features might not be available everywhere. If Cortana isn't available or is turned off, you can still use search.
Windows logo key ⊞ +D	Display and hide the desktop

Windows logo key ⊞ +E	Open File Explorer
Windows logo key ⊞ +G	Open Game bar when a game is open
Windows logo key ⊞ +H	Open the Share charm
Windows logo key ⊞ +I	Open Settings
Windows logo key ⊞ +K	Open the Connect quick action
Windows logo key ⊞ +L	Lock your PC or switch accounts
Windows logo key ⊞ +M	Minimize all windows
Windows logo key ⊞ +O	Lock device orientation
Windows logo key ⊞ +P	Choose a presentation display mode
Windows logo key ⊞ +R	Open the Run dialog box
Windows logo key ⊞ +S	Open Search
Windows logo key ⊞ +T	Cycle through apps on the taskbar
Windows logo key ⊞ +U	Open Ease of Access Center
Windows logo key ⊞ +V	Cycle through notifications
Windows logo key ⊞ +Shift+V	Cycle through notifications in reverse order

Windows logo key ⊞ +X	Open the Quick Link menu
Windows logo key ⊞ +Z	Show the commands available in an app in full-screen mode
Windows logo key ⊞ +comma (,)	Temporarily peek at the desktop
Windows logo key ⊞ +Pause	Display the System Properties dialog box
Windows logo key ⊞ +Ctrl+F	Search for PCs (if you're on a network)
Windows logo key ⊞ +Shift+M	Restore minimized windows on the desktop
Windows logo key ⊞ +number	Open the desktop and start the app pinned to the taskbar in the position indicated by the number. If the app is already running, switch to that app.
Windows logo key ⊞ +Shift+number	Open the desktop and start a new instance of the app pinned to the taskbar in the position indicated by the number
Windows logo key ⊞ +Ctrl+number	Open the desktop and switch to the last active window of the app pinned to the taskbar in the position indicated by the number
Windows logo key ⊞ +Alt+number	Open the desktop and open the Jump List for the app pinned to the taskbar in the position indicated by the number

Windows logo key ⊞ +Ctrl+Shift+number	Open the desktop and open a new instance of the app located at the given position on the taskbar as an administrator
Windows logo key ⊞ +Tab	Open Task view
Windows logo key ⊞ +Ctrl+B	Switch to the app that displayed a message in the notification area
Windows logo key ⊞ +Up arrow	Maximize the window
Windows logo key ⊞ +Down arrow	Remove current app from screen or minimize the desktop window
Windows logo key ⊞ +Left arrow	Maximize the app or desktop window to the left side of the screen
Windows logo key ⊞ +Right arrow	Maximize the app or desktop window to the right side of the screen
Windows logo key ⊞ +Home	Minimize all but the active desktop window (restores all windows on second stroke)
Windows logo key ⊞ +Shift+Up arrow	Stretch the desktop window to the top and bottom of the screen
Windows logo key ⊞ +Shift+Down arrow	Restore/minimize active desktop windows vertically, maintaining width

Windows logo key ⊞ +Shift+Left arrow or Right arrow	Move an app or window in the desktop from one monitor to another
Windows logo key ⊞ +Spacebar	Switch input language and keyboard layout
Windows logo key ⊞ +Ctrl+Spacebar	Change to a previously selected input
Windows logo key ⊞ +Enter	Open Narrator
Windows logo key ⊞ +forward slash (/)	Initiate IME reconversion
Windows logo key ⊞ +plus (+) or minus (-)	Zoom in or out using Magnifier
Windows logo key ⊞ +Esc	Exit Magnifier

Command Prompt Keyboard Shortcuts

Command Prompt also known by the following names: command-line interface, command language interpreter, console user interface and character user interface is a way of interacting with the computer program through the use of straight acceptable text (Command line).

The following table contains keyboard shortcuts that you can use in Command Prompt.

Shortcut	Action
Ctrl+C (or Ctrl+Insert)	Copy the selected text
Ctrl+V (or Shift+Insert)	Paste the selected text
Ctrl+M	Enter Mark mode
Alt+selection key	Begin selection in block mode
Arrow keys	Move the cursor in the direction specified
Page up	Move the cursor by one page up
Page down	Move the cursor by one page down
Ctrl+Home (Mark mode)	Move the cursor to the beginning of the buffer
Ctrl+End (Mark mode)	Move the cursor to the end of the buffer
Ctrl+Up arrow	Move up one line in the output history

Ctrl+Down arrow	Move down one line in the output history
Ctrl+Home (History navigation)	If the command line is empty, move the viewport to the top of the buffer. Otherwise, delete all the characters to the left of the cursor in the command line.
Ctrl+End (History navigation)	If the command line is empty, move the viewport to the command line. Otherwise, delete all the characters to the right of the cursor in the command line.

Dialog Box Keyboard Shortcuts

A small window that communicates information to the user and prompts them for a response.

The following table contains keyboard shortcuts that you can use in dialog boxes.

Shortcut	Action
F4	Display the items in the active list
Ctrl+Tab	Move forward through tabs
Ctrl+Shift+Tab	Move back through tabs
Ctrl+number (number 1-9)	Move to nth tab
Tab	Move forward through options
Shift+Tab	Move back through options
Alt+underlined letter	Perform the command (or select the option) that goes with that letter
Spacebar	Select or clear the check box if the active option is a check box
Backspace	Open a folder one level up if a folder is selected in the Save As or Open dialog box
Arrow keys	Select a button if the active option is a group of option buttons

File Explorer Keyboard Shortcuts

File Explorer is an app that comes with Microsoft windows operating system, which sees to the management of files. Its previous name was, *"Windows Explorer"*.
The presence of File Explorer makes it easy for operators to locate their files without difficulty.

The following table contains keyboard shortcuts for working with File Explorer windows or folders.

Shortcut	Action
Alt+D	Select the address bar
Ctrl+E	Select the search box
Ctrl+F	Select the search box
Ctrl+N	Open a new window
Ctrl+W	Close the current window
Ctrl+mouse scroll wheel	Change the size and appearance of file and folder icons
Ctrl+Shift+E	Display all folders above the selected folder
Ctrl+Shift+N	Create a new folder
Num Lock+asterisk (*)	Display all subfolders under the selected folder
Num Lock+plus (+)	Display the contents of the selected folder
Num Lock+minus (-)	Collapse the selected folder
Alt+P	Display the preview pane

Alt+Enter	Open the Properties dialog box for the selected item
Alt+Right arrow	View the next folder
Alt+Up arrow	View the folder that the folder was in
Alt+Left arrow	View the previous folder
Backspace	View the previous folder
Right arrow	Display the current selection (if it's collapsed), or select the first subfolder
Left arrow	Collapse the current selection (if it's expanded), or select the folder that the folder was in
End	Display the bottom of the active window
Home	Display the top of the active window
F11	Maximize or minimize the active window

Virtual Desktops Keyboard Shortcuts

A virtual desktop is an individual user's interface in a virtualized environment. The virtualized desktop is stored on a remote server rather that locally.
From ***Tech Target.***

The following table contains keyboard shortcuts for working with Virtual Desktop.

Shortcut	Action
Windows logo key ⊞ +Tab	Open Task view
Windows logo key ⊞ +Ctrl+D	Add a virtual desktop
Windows logo key ⊞ +Ctrl+Right arrow	Switch between virtual desktops you've created on the right
Windows logo key ⊞ +Ctrl+Left arrow	Switch between virtual desktops you've created on the left
Windows logo key ⊞ +Ctrl+F4	Close the virtual desktop you're using

Taskbar Keyboard Shortcuts

The *taskbar* is the long horizontal bar at the bottom of your computer screen.

The following table contains keyboard shortcuts for working with items on the desktop taskbar.

Shortcut	Action
Shift+click a taskbar button	Open an app or quickly open another instance of an app
Ctrl+Shift+click a taskbar button	Open an app as an administrator
Shift+right-click a taskbar button	Show the window menu for the app
Shift+right-click a grouped taskbar button	Show the window menu for the group
Ctrl+click a grouped taskbar button	Cycle through the windows of the group

Ease of Access Keyboard Shortcuts

The following table contains keyboard shortcuts that can help make your computer easier to use.

Shortcut	Action
Right Shift for eight seconds	Turn Filter Keys on and off
Left Alt+left Shift+Print Screen	Turn High Contrast on or off
Left Alt+left Shift+Num Lock	Turn Mouse Keys on or off
Shift five times	Turn Sticky Keys on or off
Num Lock for five seconds	Turn Toggle Keys on or off
Windows logo key ⊞+U	Open the Ease of Access Center

Magnifier Keyboard Shortcuts

Magnifier is a useful tool that enlarges part or all of your screen so you can see the words and images better. It comes with a few different settings, so you can use it the way that suits you best. Its work is to zoom in or out in order to create what the user views in different sizes.

The following table contains keyboard shortcuts for working with Magnifier.

Shortcut	Action
Windows logo key ⊞+plus (+) or minus (-)	Zoom in or out
Ctrl+Alt+Spacebar	Preview the desktop in full-screen mode
Ctrl+Alt+D	Switch to docked mode
Ctrl+Alt+F	Switch to full-screen mode
Ctrl+Alt+I	Invert colors
Ctrl+Alt+L	Switch to lens mode
Ctrl+Alt+R	Resize the lens
Ctrl+Alt+arrow keys	Pan in the direction of the arrow keys
Windows logo key ⊞+Esc	Exit Magnifier

Narrator Keyboard Shortcuts

The following table contains keyboard shortcuts for working with Narrator.

Shortcut	Action
Windows logo key ⊞ +Enter	Open Narrator
Spacebar or Enter	Activate current item
Tab and arrow keys	Move around on the screen
Ctrl	Stop reading
Caps Lock+D	Read item
Caps Lock+M	Start reading
Caps Lock+H	Read document
Caps Lock+V	Repeat phrase
Caps Lock+W	Read window
Caps Lock+Page Up or Page Down	Increase or decrease the volume of the voice
Caps Lock+plus (+) or minus (-)	Increase or decrease the speed of the voice
Caps Lock+Spacebar	Do default action
Caps Lock+Left or Right arrows	Move to previous/next item
Caps Lock+F2	Show commands for current item
Press Caps Lock twice in quick succession	Turn Caps Lock on or off
Caps+Esc	Exit Narrator

Narrator Touch Keyboard Shortcuts

This reads out the text on the screen of a windows 8.1 touch device so the user can know its content even without looking at the screen. It was added in windows 8.1 to enable those with impaired sight, the blind or such likes use the devices.

The following table contains keyboard shortcuts for working with Narrator on a four-point tablet.

Shortcut	Action
Tap once with two fingers	Stop Narrator from reading
Tap three times with four fingers	Show all Narrator commands (including the ones not in this list)
Double-tap	Activate primary action
Triple-tap	Activate secondary action
Touch or drag a single finger	Read what's under your fingers
Flick left/right with one finger	Move to next or previous item
Swipe left/right/up/down with two fingers	Scroll
Swipe down with three fingers	Start reading on explorable text

CHAPTER THREE
Windows 10 Shortcut Keys (Using Apps).

Settings Keyboard Shortcuts

The following table contains keyboard shortcuts for Settings.

Shortcut	Action
Windows logo key ⊞+I	Open settings
Backspace	Go back to the settings home page
Type on any page with search box	Search settings

Remote Desktop Keyboard Shortcuts

Remote Desktop Services (RDS), known as Terminal Services in Windows Server 2008 and earlier, is one of the components of Microsoft Windows that allows a user to take control of a **remote** computer or virtual machine over a network **connection.**

With *Remote Desktop Connection*, you can sit at a PC and connect to another PC in a different location (the *remote* PC). For example, you can sit at your home PC and connect to your work PC, and use all of your apps, files, and network resources as if you were sitting right in front of your work PC.

The following table contains keyboard shortcuts for working with Remote Desktop Connection on the desktop.

Shortcut	Action
Ctrl+Alt+Insert	Scroll
Ctrl+Alt+Left/Right arrow	Switch between sessions
Ctrl+Alt+Up/Down arrow	View the session selection bar
Ctrl+Alt+Home	In full-screen mode, view connection options

Microsoft Edge Keyboard Shortcuts

This is the default browser of windows 10, previously called by its code name "Project Spartan". Microsoft Edge has features such as built in notetaking, sharing and Cortana digital assistant.

The following are Microsoft Edge keyboard shortcuts

Shortcut	Action
Ctrl+D	Add current site to favorites or reading list
Ctrl+I	Open favorites pane
Ctrl+J	Open downloads pane
Ctrl+H	Open history pane
Ctrl+P	Print the current page
Ctrl+F	Find on page
Alt+C	Open Cortana **Note** • Cortana is only available in certain countries/regions, and some Cortana features might not be available everywhere. If Cortana isn't available or is turned off, you can still use search.

Ctrl+Shift+R	Enter reading view
F12	Open F12 Developer Tools
F7	Turn caret browsing on for the current tab
Ctrl+Shift+Delete	Open clear browsing data pane
Ctrl+T	Open a new tab
Ctrl+Shift+T	Reopen the last closed tab
Ctrl+W or Ctrl+F4	Close current tab
Ctrl+K	Duplicate tab
Ctrl+N	Open a new window
Ctrl+Shift+P	Open a new InPrivate Browsing window
Ctrl+Tab	Switch to the next tab
Ctrl+Shift+Tab	Switch to the previous tab
Ctrl+1, 2, 3,…, 8	Switch to a specific tab number
Ctrl+9	Switch to the last tab
Ctrl+plus (+)	Zoom in (25%)
Ctrl+minus (-)	Zoom out (25%)
Ctrl+0	Reset zoom level
Backspace or Alt+Left arrow	Go back
Alt+Right arrow	Go forward
F5 or Ctrl+R	Refresh the page
Esc	Stop loading the page
Ctrl+L or F4 or Alt+D	Select the address bar
Ctrl+Shift+L	Open address bar query in a new tab
Ctrl+E	Open a search query in the address bar

Ctrl+Enter	Add www. to the beginning and .com to the end of text typed in the address bar
Ctrl+click	Open link in a new tab
Ctrl+Shift+click	Open link in a new tab and switch to the tab
Alt+Shift+click	Open link in a new window

Game Bar Keyboard Shortcuts

The following table contains keyboard shortcuts for using the Game Bar.

Shortcut	Action
Windows logo key ⊞ +G	Open Game bar when a game is open
Windows logo key ⊞ +Alt+G	Record the last 30 seconds
Windows logo key ⊞ +Alt+R	Start recording (press the shortcut again to stop recording)
Windows logo key ⊞ +Alt+Print Screen	Take a screenshot of your game
Windows logo key ⊞ +Alt+T	Show/hide recording timer

Photos App Keyboard Shortcuts

The following table contains keyboard shortcuts for working with Photos Apps.

Shortcut	Action
Windows logo key ⊞+H	Open the Share charm
Spacebar (in Collection)	Select an item and enter Selection mode
Enter (from Selection mode)	Select an item while in Selection mode
Spacebar (viewing a photo)	Show or hide commands
Spacebar (viewing a video)	Play or pause the video
Arrow keys (in Collection)	Scroll up, down, left, or right
Left or right arrow keys (viewing an item)	Show the next or previous item
Arrow keys	Move within a zoomed photo
Ctrl+plus (+)	Zoom in when viewing a photo
Ctrl+minus (-)	Zoom out when viewing a photo
Ctrl+0	Reset zoom on a photo
Esc	Return to previous screen
Ctrl+S	Save
Ctrl+P	Print
Ctrl+C	Copy
Ctrl+R (viewing or editing)	Rotate a photo
E (viewing a photo)	Enhance a photo

Ctrl+Z (editing)	Undo changes
Ctrl+Y (editing)	Redo changes
Ctrl+forward slash (/) (editing)	View original
Shift+arrow keys	Resize crop or selective focus area
Ctrl+arrow keys	Move crop or selective focus area
F5 (viewing an item)	Start a slide show
Alt+Enter	View file info
Ctrl+L	Set as lock screen

Calculator Keyboard Shortcuts

A component of *Microsoft* Windows used for Math work accounting and other related operations.

The following table contains keyboard shortcuts for working with Calculator.

Shortcut	Action
Alt+1	Switch to Standard mode
Alt+2	Switch to Scientific mode
Alt+3	Switch to Programmer mode
Ctrl+M	Store in memory
Ctrl+P	Add to memory
Ctrl+Q	Subtract from memory
Ctrl+R	Recall from memory
Ctrl+L	Clear memory
F9	Select ±
R	Select 1/x
@	Calculate the square root
Del	Select CE
Ctrl+H	Turn calculation history on or off
Up arrow	Move up in history list
Down arrow	Move down in history list
Ctrl+Shift+D	Clear history
F3	Select DEG in Scientific mode
F4	Select RAD in Scientific mode
F5	Select GRAD in Scientific mode

Ctrl+G	Select 10^x in Scientific mode
Ctrl+O	Select cosh in Scientific mode
Ctrl+S	Select sinh in Scientific mode
Ctrl+T	Select tanh in Scientific mode
Shift+S	Select sin-1 in Scientific mode
Shift+O	Select cos-1 in Scientific mode
Shift+T	Select tan-1 in Scientific mode
Ctrl+Y	Select y√x in Scientific mode
D	Select Mod in Scientific mode
L	Select log in Scientific mode
M	Select dms in Scientific mode
N	Select ln in Scientific mode
Ctrl+N	Select e^x in Scientific mode
O	Select cos in Scientific mode
P	Select Pi in Scientific mode
Q	Select x^2 in Scientific mode
S	Select sin in Scientific mode
T	Select tan in Scientific mode
V	Select F-E in Scientific mode
X	Select Exp in Scientific mode
Y, ^	Select x^y in Scientific mode
#	Select x^3 in Scientific mode
;	Select Int in Scientific mode
!	Select n! in Scientific mode
F2	Select DWORD in Programmer mode
F3	Sclect WORD in Programmer mode
F4	Select BYTE in Programmer mode
F5	Select HEX in Programmer mode
F6	Select DEC in Programmer mode
F7	Select OCT in Programmer mode

F8	Select BIN in Programmer mode
F12	Select QWORD in Programmer mode
A-F	Select A-F in Programmer mode
J	Select RoL in Programmer mode
K	Select RoR in Programmer mode
<	Select Lsh in Programmer mode
>	Select Rsh in Programmer mode
%	Select Mod in Programmer mode
|	Select Or in Programmer mode
^	Select Xor in Programmer mode
~	Select Not in Programmer mode
&	Select And in Programmer mode
Spacebar	Toggle the bit value in Programmer mode

Reader Keyboard Shortcuts

Reader, as the name suggests is a Microsoft reading app that opens PDF, XPS and TIFF files, it enables user to take notes or fill forms, print or share its content with others.

The following table contains keyboard shortcuts for working with the Reader app.

Shortcut	Action
F8	Use two-page layout
Ctrl+R	Rotate the file 90 degrees clockwise
Ctrl+F	Search for text in a file
F7	Use keyboard selection mode
Ctrl+P	Print a file
Ctrl+O	Open a file
Ctrl+W	Close a file
Ctrl+M	Reader app home

Paint Keyboard Shortcuts

Microsoft Paint or '*MS Paint*' is a basic graphics or *painting* utility that is included in all the *Microsoft* Windows versions. *MS Paint* can be used to draw, colour and edit pictures, including imported pictures from a digital camera for example. *MS Paint* is found in the Windows Start menu within the Accessories Folder.

The following table contains keyboard shortcuts for working with Paint.

Shortcut	Action
F11	View a picture in full-screen mode
F12	Save the picture as a new file
Ctrl+A	Select the entire picture
Ctrl+B	Bold selected text
Ctrl+C	Copy a selection to the Clipboard
Ctrl+E	Open the Properties dialog box
Ctrl+G	Show or hide gridlines
Ctrl+I	Italicize selected text
Ctrl+N	Create a new picture
Ctrl+O	Open an existing picture
Ctrl+P	Print a picture
Ctrl+R	Show or hide the ruler
Ctrl+S	Save changes to a picture
Ctrl+U	Underline selected text
Ctrl+V	Paste a selection from the Clipboard
Ctrl+W	Open the Resize and Skew dialog box
Ctrl+X	Cut a selection
Ctrl+Y	Redo a change

Ctrl+Z	Undo a change
Ctrl+plus (+)	Increase the width of a brush, line, or shape outline by one pixel
Ctrl+minus (-)	Decrease the width of a brush, line, or shape outline by one pixel
Ctrl+Page Up	Zoom in
Ctrl+Page Down	Zoom out
Alt (or F10)	Display keytips
Alt+F4	Close a picture and its Paint window
Right arrow	Move the selection or active shape right by one pixel
Left arrow	Move the selection or active shape left by one pixel
Down arrow	Move the selection or active shape down by one pixel
Up arrow	Move the selection or active shape up by one pixel
Shift+F10	Show the current shortcut menu

Windows Journal Keyboard Shortcuts

Windows Journal is a notetaking application, created by Microsoft and included in Windows XP Tablet PC Edition as well as the Home Premium or superior.

The following table contains keyboard shortcuts for working with Windows Journal.

Shortcut	Action
F5	Refresh the note list
F6	Toggle between a note list and a note
F11	View a note in full-screen mode
Ctrl+A	Select all items on a page
Ctrl+C	Copy a selection to the Clipboard
Ctrl+F	Search for text in a file
Ctrl+G	Go to a page
Ctrl+N	Start a new note
Ctrl+O	Open a recently used note
Ctrl+P	Print a note
Ctrl+S	Save changes to a note
Ctrl+V	Paste a selection from the Clipboard
Ctrl+X	Cut a selection
Ctrl+Y	Redo a change
Ctrl+Z	Undo a change
Alt+F4	Close a note and its Journal window
Ctrl+Shift+C	Display a shortcut menu for column headings in a note list
Ctrl+Shift+V	Move a note to a specific folder

WordPad Keyboard Shortcuts

WordPad is a basic word processor that is included with almost all versions of **Microsoft** Windows from Windows 95 onwards. It is more advanced than Notepad but simpler than **Microsoft** Word.

It is a text-editing program you can use to create and edit documents

The following table contains keyboard shortcuts for working with WordPad.

Shortcut	Action
F3	Search for the next instance of the text in the Find dialog box
F10	Display keytips
F12	Save the document as a new file
Ctrl+1	Set single line spacing
Ctrl+2	Set double line spacing
Ctrl+5	Set line spacing to 1.5
Ctrl+A	Select the entire document
Ctrl+B	Make selected text bold
Ctrl+C	Copy a selection to the Clipboard
Ctrl+D	Insert a Microsoft Paint drawing
Ctrl+E	Align text center
Ctrl+F	Search for text in a document
Ctrl+H	Replace text in a document
Ctrl+I	Italicize selected text

Ctrl+J	Justify text
Ctrl+L	Align text left
Ctrl+N	Create a new document
Ctrl+O	Open an existing document
Ctrl+P	Print a document
Ctrl+R	Align text right
Ctrl+S	Save changes to a document
Ctrl+U	Underline selected text
Ctrl+V	Paste a selection from the Clipboard
Ctrl+X	Cut a selection
Ctrl+Y	Redo a change
Ctrl+Z	Undo a change
Ctrl+equal (=)	Make selected text subscript
Ctrl+Shift+equal (=)	Make selected text superscript
Ctrl+Shift+greater than (>)	Increase the font size
Ctrl+Shift+less than (<)	Decrease the font size
Ctrl+Shift+A	Change characters to all capitals
Ctrl+Shift+L	Change the bullet style
Ctrl+Left arrow	Move the cursor one word to the left
Ctrl+Right arrow	Move the cursor one word to the right
Ctrl+Up arrow	Move the cursor to the previous line
Ctrl+Down arrow	Move the cursor to the next line

Ctrl+Home	Move to the beginning of the document
Ctrl+End	Move to the end of the document
Ctrl+Page Up	Move up one page
Ctrl+Page Down	Move down one page
Ctrl+Delete	Delete the next word
Alt+F4	Close WordPad
Shift+F10	Show the current shortcut menu

JUST BEFORE YOU PUT ME DOWN, NOTE THIS.

i.   The plus (+) signs that come in the middle of the keyboard shortcuts simply means the keys are meant to be combined or one held down while pressing the other (s), it is not to be added as one of the shortcut keys, and in a case where plus sign is needed, it will be duplicated or written twice (++) in that shortcut column.

ii.   For keyboard shortcuts in which you press one key immediately followed by another key, the keys are separated by a comma (,).

iii. Most programs also provide accelerator keys that can make it easier to work with menus and other commands. Check the menus of programs for accelerator keys. If a letter is underlined in a menu that usually means that pressing the Alt key in combination with the underlined key will have the same effect as clicking that menu item.

iv.   Pressing the Alt key in some programs, such as Paint and WordPad, shows commands that are labeled with additional keys that you can press to use them.

v.   **Highlight** is the same thing as **select** in this book.

vi. **"Shortcut"** here means the key combination to be used in order to achieve a particular result and **"Action"** stands for the outcome of the key or combined keys.

Customer's Page.

This page is for customers who enjoyed Windows 10 Shortcut Keys.

Dearly beloved customer, please leave a review behind if you enjoyed this book or found it helpful. It will be highly appreciated, thank you.

Download Our Free EBooks Today From your Favourite Bookstore.

In order to appreciate our customers who ceaselessly patronize us, we have made some of our titles available at 0.00. They are totally free. Feel free to get a copy of the free titles.

(A) For Keyboard Shortcuts In Windows

Go to Amazon: Windows 7 Keyboard shortcuts

Go to Other Digital Stores: Windows 7 Keyboard Shortcuts

(B) For Keyboard Shortcuts In Office 2016 for Windows.

Go to Amazon: Word 2016 Keyboard Shortcuts For windows

Go to Other Digital Stores: Word 2016 Keyboard Shortcuts For Windows

(C) For Keyboard Shortcuts In Office 2016 for Mac.

Go to Amazon: OneNote 2016 Keyboard Shortcuts For Macintosh

Go to Other Digital Stores: OneNote 2016 Keyboard Shortcuts For Macintosh

Note: Feel free to download them from your favorite store today. Thank you!

Other Books By This Publisher.

S/N	Title	Series
Series A: Limits Breaking Quotes.		
1	Discover Your Key Christian Quotes	Limits Breaking Quotes
Series B: Shortcut Matters.		
1	Windows 7 Shortcuts	Shortcut Matters

2	Windows 7 Shortcuts & Tips	Shortcut Matters
3	Windows 8.1 Shortcuts	Shortcut Matters
4	Windows 10 Shortcut Keys	Shortcut Matters
5	Microsoft Office 2007 Keyboard Shortcuts For Windows.	Shortcut Matters
6	Microsoft Office 2010 Shortcuts For Windows.	Shortcut Matters
7	Microsoft Office 2013 Shortcuts For Windows.	Shortcut Matters
8	Microsoft Office 2016 Shortcuts For Windows.	Shortcut Matters
9	Microsoft Office 2016 Keyboard Shortcuts For Macintosh.	Shortcut Matters
10	Top 11 Adobe Programs Keyboard Shortcuts	Shortcut Matters
11	Top 10 Email Clients Keyboard Shortcuts	Shortcut Matters
12	Hot Corel Programs Keyboard Shortcuts	Shortcut Matters
13	Top 10 Browsers Keyboard Shortcuts	Shortcut Matters

Series C: Teach Yourself.

1	Teach Yourself Computer Fundamentals	Teach Yourself

Series D: For Painless Publishing

1	Self-Publish it with CreateSpace.	For Painless Publishing

2	Where is my money? Now solved for Kindle and CreateSpace	For Painless Publishing
3	Describe it on Amazon	For Painless Publishing
4	How To Market That Book.	For Painless Publishing